BATTLE BRIEFINGS

GETTYSBURG

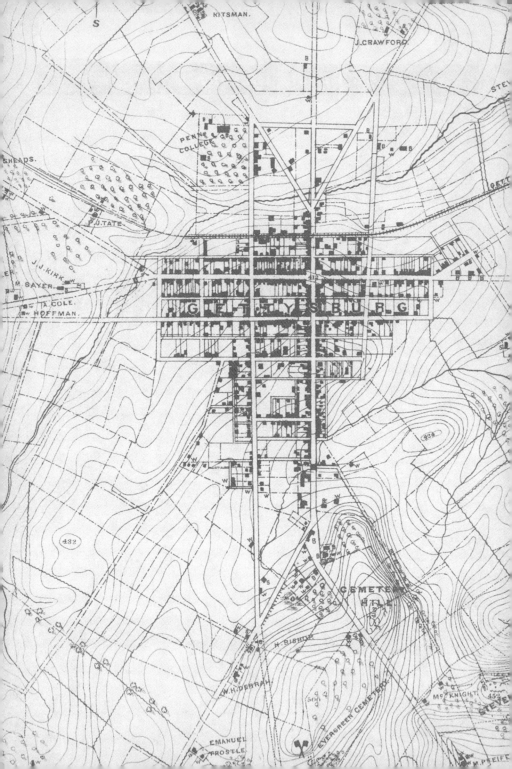

BATTLE BRIEFINGS

GETTYSBURG

Thomas R. Flagel

STACKPOLE
BOOKS

Guilford, Connecticut

STACKPOLE BOOKS

Published by Stackpole Books
An imprint of The Rowman & Littlefield Publishing Group, Inc.
4501 Forbes Blvd., Ste. 200
Lanham, MD 20706
www.rowman.com

Distributed by NATIONAL BOOK NETWORK
800-462-6420

British Library Cataloguing in Publication Information available

Library of Congress Cataloging-in-Publication Data

Names: Flagel, Thomas R., 1966– author.
Title: Gettysburg / Thomas R. Flagel.
Description: Guilford, Connecticut : Stackpole Books, [2019] | Series: Battle
  briefings | Includes bibliographical references.
Identifiers: LCCN 2018054398 (print) | LCCN 2019000795 (ebook) | ISBN
  9780811767859 | ISBN 9780811736633 (pbk. : alk. paper) | ISBN
  9780811767859 (e-book)
Subjects: LCSH: Gettysburg, Battle of, Gettysburg, Pa., 1863.
Classification: LCC E475.53 (ebook) | LCC E475.53 .F579 2019 (print) | DDC
  973.7/349—dc23
LC record available at https://lccn.loc.gov/2018054398

♾™ The paper used in this publication meets the minimum requirements of
American National Standard for Information Sciences—Permanence of Paper for
Printed Library Materials, ANSI/NISO Z39.48-1992.

Printed in the United States of America

Contents

Series Introduction

FOR MORE THAN NINETY YEARS, STACKPOLE BOOKS has been publishing the very best in military history, from ancient Rome to the modern Middle East, from foxhole to headquarters. We are proud to draw on that rich heritage—our decades of experience and expertise—in publishing this brand-new series, Battle Briefings. Intended as short overviews, these books aim to introduce readers to history's most important battles and campaigns—and, we hope, to provide a launching pad for further exploration of the endlessly fascinating nooks and crannies of military history.

Introduction

THIS BRIEFING IS WRITTEN IN THE historical present, also known as the narrative present, to illustrate the hopes, anxieties, suppositions, and confusion intrinsic within such monumental and traumatic events. Most place names will be absent or vague, as they were to the multitudes of soldiers seeing Gettysburg for the first time. For the civilian perspective, the text quotes eyewitness and newspaper accounts, including actual rumors that appeared in newsprint during the campaign. The reader will still be privy to far more information than the combatants and general populace received at the time, but the reader will also gain an opportunity for empathy. In short, those living in 1863 were much like we are today—human beings trying to navigate a complex present into an uncertain future.

Events up to Spring 1863

Nov 6, 1860	Abraham Lincoln elected; most Deep South whites oppose
Dec 20, 1860	South Carolina convention declares secession; six more states soon follow
Feb 18, 1861	Jefferson Davis inaugurated provisional Confederate president
March 4, 1861	Lincoln inaugurated
April 12, 1861	South Carolina shells Fort Sumter
April 15, 1861	Lincoln calls for 75,000 volunteers; Davis soon calls for 200,000
April–June, 1861	Four more state governments declare secession
July 21, 1861	First major battle—Manassas, VA
Aug 5, 1861	Union creates national income tax to pay for war
Aug 1861	War escalates in Missouri and Kentucky
Feb 1862	Union begins to retake Mississippi, Cumberland, and Tennessee Rivers
Feb 25, 1862	U.S. Congress makes greenbacks legal tender to restart economy
Feb–May 1862	Union retakes Nashville and much of Tennessee
March 1862	War escalates in Arkansas

(continued)

Events up to Spring 1863

March 9, 1862	Birth of ironclad combat at Hampton Roads, VA
April 6–7, 1862	Battle of Shiloh, TN—first major bloodbath of war
April 16, 1862	Confederate Congress first to enact military draft
April 25, 1862	Union retakes New Orleans
May 20, 1862	U.S. Congress passes Homestead Act aiding migration to Midwest
July 1, 1862	U.S. Congress funds transcontinental railroad
July 2, 1862	U.S. Congress passes Land Grant Act to create engineering colleges
Sept 17, 1862	Battle of Antietam, MD—bloodiest battle to date
Sept 1862	Confederates retake much of Tennessee
Sept 22, 1862	Lincoln announces Emancipation Proclamation
Oct 8, 1862	Battle of Perryville, KY, reverses Confederate gains in region
Nov 1862	Slave escapes to Union areas escalate
Jan 1, 1863	Emancipation Proclamation becomes official
April 1863	Bread riots in several Confederate cities
May 1863	Battle of Chancellorsville, VA—Stonewall Jackson mortally wounded
May 18, 1863	Union siege of Vicksburg, MS, begins

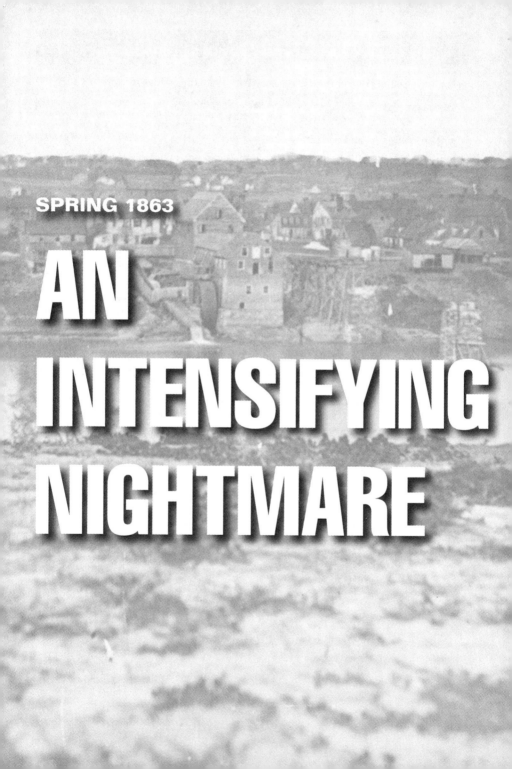

SPRING 1863

AN INTENSIFYING NIGHTMARE

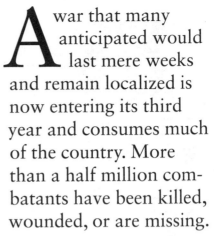

A war that many anticipated would last mere weeks and remain localized is now entering its third year and consumes much of the country. More than a half million combatants have been killed, wounded, or are missing.

Time and again, this conflict threatens to metastasize even further, into British North America and Mexico. It already rages on the seas. The Union blockade has grown to four hundred ships, Confederate privateers harass Union merchant vessels from the Caribbean to Burma, and feudal lords in Japan are threatening to shell any U.S. craft that approaches their shores. This looks increasingly like a world war in the making, and at home there is no end in sight.[1]

The worst of the fighting is midway between the Union and Confederate capitals. The two largest field armies in the world—the Army of the Potomac and the Army of Northern Virginia—have sparred in a series of massive and morbid battles, only to find themselves deadlocked along the "Dare Mark" of the Rappahannock River. A faint hope prevails that some

great unforeseen event will end this horrific contest once and for all, but at present, leaders among both warring parties have the haunting suspicion that their own side is losing.

For the North, despite its considerable industrial, financial, and military superiority, the push toward Richmond seems to yield nothing but misery. Last autumn, a ghastly battle in Maryland created the bloodiest day of the war to date. When unprecedented photographs of the combat fatalities went public, even the most ardent Unionists began to wonder if this whole struggle was worth the cost. Just three months later, waves of Federals charged the heights outside Fredericksburg, a mere fifty miles from Washington, only to produce the second bloodiest day in the nation's history and the government's most lopsided defeat to date.

My God, my God. What will the country say?[2]
➤ *Lincoln after the severe Union defeat at Fredericksburg*

The collective carnage necessitated Congress to establish a new entity called "national cemeteries" to house their ever-growing numbers of dead. Just fifteen years ago, the United States military traversed

AN INTENSIFYING NIGHTMARE

Fredericksburg, Virginia, three months after the eponymous battle that claimed 17,900 dead and wounded along the "Dare Mark" between Union- and Confederate-occupied territories.

thousands of miles, scored a series of crushing victories, and entered triumphant into the halls of Montezuma. Today, an army far larger than the one that defeated Mexico can hardly manage to hold obscure towns within marching distance of its own national capital.

The horizon is just as dark for secessionists, for whom the occasional stunning upset shines only briefly. Since the spring of 1862, Federals have regained most of Missouri, Kentucky, and Arkansas, and occupy Memphis, New Orleans, and Nashville. In the past few months, the Union Army has been constructing a chain of forts along the Cumberland, Mississippi, and Tennessee Rivers, to which the nearby enslaved are escaping in droves. Bread riots plague the cities.[3] The besieged citadel of Vicksburg is on the verge of surrender. Its loss will almost certainly split the Confederacy in two.

General Robert Edward Lee

Commander, Army of Northern Virginia

Age: 56

Nicknames: Marse Robert, Granny Lee, the Old Man, King of Spades

Health: Fatigue, shortness of breath, chest pains. May have suffered a heart attack during the Battle of Chancellorsville.

Military Experience: West Point graduate (1840), Mexican War, Native wars, multiple battles in the Eastern Theater.

Strengths: Reputation as the ablest and most successful general on either side. Adored by his men and the Confederate public. President Jefferson Davis expresses virtually limitless faith in him. Ability to anticipate actions of opponents.

Weaknesses: Tends to give vague orders. His battles often result in enormous casualties for his own side. Death of Stonewall Jackson has left him without his ablest combat general. Virginia-centric in his strategies and loyalties. ■

It is this last crisis that prompts Jefferson Davis to seek a solution from the seemingly invincible Gen. Robert E. Lee, who has apparently arrived in Richmond to meet with Davis and his cabinet. Will Davis send his vaunted Army of Northern Virginia westward to rescue Vicksburg, or at the very least save the sinking Tennessee Valley? The day has come when it seems only the venerable Lee can hold the Confederate experiment together.

June 3

The Army of Northern Virginia has quietly slipped away from the banks of the Rappahannock, and the Army of the Potomac has lost contact. Maj. Gen. "Fighting Joe" Hooker is begging his War Department for permission to cross the Rappahannock to investigate, but his commander-in-chief is vetoing the idea.

Gen. Robert Edward Lee. BRADY-HANDY PHOTOGRAPH COLLECTION, LIBRARY OF CONGRESS

I would not take any risk of being entangled upon the river, like an ox jumped half over a fence, and liable to be torn by dogs.[4]

> ➤ *Lincoln telegraph to Hooker*

Consequently, no one knows where Lee is heading, perhaps including Lee himself. Ever the opportunist, Marse Robert could be leading his men anywhere the compass points. The newspapers certainly think so. New York's gossipy *Herald* is telling its readers that the Virginian intends to capture Harrisburg or Philadelphia.[5] The *Memphis Appeal*, printing on the run in Atlanta, says his destination is Wheeling or Pittsburgh.[6] In the District of Columbia, editors of the *Alexandria Gazette* believe Lee is either moving southwest or solidifying his position in Virginia, with designs on Washington if the opportunity arises.[7]

The plans of Lee are still a secret to our enemies, as well as to ourselves.[8]

> ➤ Richmond Enquirer,
> *July 3, 1863*

While others guess, the *Mobile Register* jests: "We are unable to find the remotest clue to his [Lee's]

intentions in any of his movements, and are prepared to be surprised by nothing that happens—whether he alights from a balloon in the park of New York City, sweeps like an eagle upon Grant in the great valley, or sails up the Mississippi River on board of the fleet built for the Emperor of China."[9] The Alabama daily's editors can sport a sense of humor because their readers are not in the path of the storm.

Friend or foe, anyone living within the trajectory of these now mobile behemoths must worry. Each army numbers in excess of 70,000—greater than the population of Pittsburgh—with appetites for food, forage, livestock, and lodging to match. A single corps alone can occupy twenty miles of road and devour several tons of food and fodder each day. If the armies meet, their combined population will make them the ninth largest city in the country.

One certainty the American public has learned from this war— there is no such thing as a "battlefield." Firefights occur on farms and among houses, around depots and within towns. Schools and courthouses become headquarters. Churches and homes become hospitals. Gardens are stripped clean and replanted with bodies. As these armies move once again, there is reason to be deathly afraid if they

AN INTENSIFYING NIGHTMARE

come to blows. Engagements have been getting larger and costlier, and Lee's movements foretell another bloodletting. Of the war's six deadliest battles so far, Lee has been involved in four of them.

June 9

It is confirmed. The Army of Northern Virginia is on the move and heading northwest. Federal cavalry stumbled upon 10,000 Confederate horsemen about twenty-five miles northwest of Fredericksburg and have been fighting for nearly ten hours. There appear to be light casualties on both sides so far.

Lincoln is taking no chances. He is drawing up orders to have 100,000 militia report for duty in Maryland, Ohio, Pennsylvania, and West Virginia. A few thousand Federal soldiers hold positions at Harpers Ferry and Winchester, but they have little chance of fending off the numbers heading their way.[10]

June 17

Reports confirm that the Army of Northern Virginia is crossing the Potomac into Maryland and heading north. Their objective is still unknown, but the route is no longer in question. Lee's men are filtering

through the Shenandoah, shielded in its wide valley, and can defend or strike through any gap they so choose.

Major General Hooker wonders if the Confederates are going to turn west and reclaim Tennessee, but citizens to the north and east are starting to panic. The city of Baltimore is commandeering slaves to build defenses. Civilians are clogging the roads from Harrisburg to Philadelphia, lugging their children and driving livestock. Most distressed are tens of thousands of free blacks in the region who fear being captured and sold into bondage. Washington and a contemplative Hooker seem unable or unwilling to help.[11]

The sudden movement of General Lee to transfer the seat of war from Virginia to Maryland or Pennsylvania makes us look forward to next news from America with deep anxiety.[12]

➤ Caledonian Mercury,
Edinburgh, Scotland, July 1, 1863

June 21

Confederates are entering Pennsylvania via the Shenandoah. Their strength is at least 60,000, although some reports say it may be closer to

100,000 or even 150,000. Hooker may have 90,000 at his disposal, now crawling to intercept. Whatever their disposition, the Confederates are entering a land of plenty. Whatever his intention, Lee can conceivably remain in the North for months.[13]

I have never yet seen any country in such a high state of cultivation. Such wheat I never dreamed of, and so much of it.[14]

> *Confederate soldier crossing into Pennsylvania*

The Keystone State is rich in horses, coal, iron, newly discovered rock oil, blacksmiths, shoemakers, clothing factories, thousands of grist mills, scores of arms manufacturers, hundreds of saddlemakers, and at least thirty-four gunpowder factories. Fields are crowded with milk cows, beef cattle, sheep, and more than a million hogs. There may be more corn and wheat grown here than in the entire Deep South combined, and enough potatoes to provide two bushels to every man, woman, and child living in the Confederacy. Even the local and state banks are lush; Pennsylvania banks hold more than three times the specie and deposits in all the depositories of Old Dominion.[15]

But this is not just a scavenging expedition. One does not bring an entire army, with hundreds of artillery pieces and long trains of ammunition, just to search for material wealth and foodstuffs.

June 27

By direction of the President, Maj. Gen. Joseph Hooker is relieved from command of the Army of the Potomac, and Maj. Gen. George G. Meade is appointed to the command.[16]

> *U.S. War Department General Orders*

The North is in peril and Lincoln has just sacked his commanding general. Considering that Meade has never expressed a desire for the position, and that the exact whereabouts and strength of the Confederates remain unknown, Meade may view the message as a curse more than a promotion. He is an able organizer but hardly charismatic. One wonders how he will inspire the men.

R.E. Lee General Orders No. 72

June 21st, 1863

While in the enemy's country, the following regulations for procuring supplies will be strictly observed . . .

I. No private property shall be injured or destroyed by any person belonging to or connected with the army, or taken, except by the officers hereinafter designated.

II. Chiefs of the Commissary, Quartermaster, Ordnance and Medical Departments of the Army will make requisitions upon the local authorities or inhabitants for the necessary supplies for their respective departments, designating the places and times of delivery. All persons complying with such requisitions shall be paid the market price [in Confederate scrip] for the articles furnished . . .

III. Should the authorities or inhabitants neglect or refuse to comply with such requisitions, the supplies required will be taken from the nearest inhabitants so refusing. ∎

Corps and other commanders are authorized to order the instant death of any soldier who fails in his duty at this hour.[17]

➤ *Meade to the Army of the Potomac*

June 29

While Meade grapples with his new appointment, the Confederate mass is pouring out of the Shenandoah and definitely heading east, elongating as it progresses, like an enormous serpent emerging from a forest. Hidden for weeks in the valley, it now lurches with jaws agape, as if to sink its fangs into the heart of the state. It may be the start of a journey to the sea.

Lee's directive to confiscate property in a civil manner has done little to spare the towns and hollows in his path. His men have traveled some two hundred circuitous miles from Fredericksburg and have thus far encountered little resistance. Their unchecked progress, plus the excitement of being in enemy country, have incited many of them to be less than conciliatory to the locals. Case in point, residents of Mercersburg were given less than a day to furnish several tons of bacon, many barrels of flour, hundreds of horses, and piles of serviceable outerwear,

Major General George Gordon Meade

Commander, Army of the Potomac

Age: 47

Nickname: Old Snapping Turtle

Health: Severe bullet wound in the hip from Battle of White Oak Swamp (1862).

Military Experience: West Point graduate (1835), Mexican War, Seminole War, multiple battles in the Eastern Theater.

Strengths: Calculating, apolitical, pragmatic, favors consensus over coercion. Strong training in artillery, engineering, infantry, and topography. Born in Spain, he cannot become president, which relieves many Unionists who are weary of generals with political ambitions.

Weaknesses: Quick temper. Has only been at the helm of the Army of the Potomac for a matter of hours. ∎

---

or have all private homes be subject to quartering. Other places see their dry goods stores gutted, barns emptied, and apothecaries raided. Some villages are given little more than worthless receipts for their losses; this occurs repeatedly as regiments move in successive waves.[18]

We passed through some of the prettiest country that I ever saw in my life . . . and some of the ugliest women.[19]

> ➢ *Confederate soldier marching*
> *toward Harrisburg*

So far, this unnerving campaign has lasted for almost a month, across four states including newly created West Virginia, igniting no fewer than two pitched battles, three heavy actions, and multitudes of separate skirmishes. At this time, the creature measures over sixty miles long. Prodding the countryside in search of it, Union Brigadier John Buford's cavalry division has stumbled into its midsection, and the mighty serpent reflexively coils. Point of contact: five miles northwest of a place called Gettysburg.

AN INTENSIFYING NIGHTMARE

Maj. Gen. George Gordon Meade.

AN INTENSIFYING NIGHTMARE

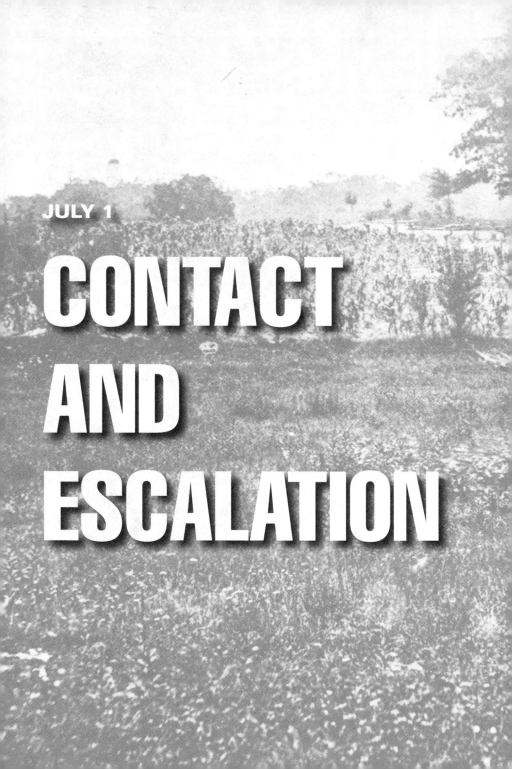

JULY 1

CONTACT AND ESCALATION

All following times are approximate.

Shots fired. Confederate infantry of unknown quantity are engaging a division of Federal cavalry west of town, and the terrain upon which they are fighting threatens to press them tightly together. In their advance, the grays are crossing a series of ridges, which alternately provide them high ground in front and hide their numbers to the rear.

The Union cavalry hold an advantage in rate of fire, armed as they are with light, mobile artillery and quick-firing carbines, but their collective range is dangerously limited. The Confederates edge ever closer and with increasing numbers. This is going to be more than a skirmish, and presently the Union side is outnumbered and outgunned.

8:00 AM

The Federals are starting to fall back. The latest news is that their only immediate support—the 8,000-strong First Corps—is still four miles away to the south, marching fast but on a poor route. Their problem is that Gettysburg is essentially a hub on a spoked-wheel

BATTLE FIELD OF GETTYSBURG.

Surveyed and drawn by the U.S. Army Corps of Engineers from 1868 to 1873, the above map closely represents the Gettysburg area landscape of July 1863.

Lutheran Theological Seminary at Gettysburg

network of roads. Lee's men are on four pikes angling directly to the site of engagement. The Federals are on just two, and the First Corps is on neither—it is marching up Emmitsburg Road, heading northeast into town and partially away from the action.

The Federal infantry will either need to enter the borough and use

it as a defensive position or head cross-country and try to rescue their cavalry on open ground.

8:30 AM

Lead regiments of the mighty Union First Corps are still two miles from Gettysburg. Civilians are fleeing south and east in ever-greater numbers; some are carrying all they can, others are running with just the clothes on their backs. Most of them are women and children.

There came a screech and a shell brushed my skirt as it went by. I staggered from the concussion of it and almost fell when I was grasped by the arm and a man said pleasantly, "That was a close call."[1]

> *Gettysburg resident Sadie Bushman, age 10*

9:00 AM

The First Corps is veering off the Emmitsburg Road and slashing their way overland toward the sound of the gunfire. The men are hacking down rail fences and pushing over stone walls, trampling through grain fields and winding through groves. Their advance is painfully slow and draining, and they are already exhausted from marching through the night.

9:30 AM

The Federals are rallying, thanks in part to the arrival of the famous Maj. Gen. John F. Reynolds. This forty-two-year-old Pennsylvania native and West Pointer has served in the military for decades, from Oregon to Mexico to Florida and a multitude of places in between. If only Lincoln would have given Reynolds free reign from political interference, the general would have accepted the president's recent offer to head the Army of the Potomac.

Still, this stalwart and tall commander is essentially second in command, and he is throwing the best of his corps directly into the fight. Among his weapons is the famed Iron Brigade, battle-hardened veterans from Wisconsin, Indiana, and Michigan.

Major General John Reynolds

U.S. Second in Command

Age: 42

Nickname: Old Common Sense

Health: Considerable mental, emotional, and physical endurance.

Military Experience: West Point graduate (1841), Mexican War, frontier fortifications across the North American continent, Mormon Wars, multiple battles in the Eastern Theater.

Strengths: Intelligent, tall and imposing, serious, respected in and out of the military. Exceptional situational awareness in combat. Pennsylvania born, which could further motivate him to fight well on home soil.

Weaknesses: Arguably too aggressive, although his personal courage tends to motivate his subordinates. ■

10:30 AM

Maj. Gen. John Reynolds is dead. His demise came when hundreds of Confederates thundered from the shadows of thick woods, firing and charging upon his position. Reynolds wheeled his mount to the rear, shouting for reinforcements, when a bullet slammed into the back of his skull. Reportedly his last words were, "Forward for God's sake and drive those fellows out of those woods."[2]

The mottled terrain is now producing fierce and costly close-quarter fighting. Both sides are struggling to stay organized, and both are pulling more units into the fray.

The Confederates are gaining ground.

Maj. Gen. John Reynolds.

Looking east-southeast where fierce fighting transpired on July 1. Center left is the Lutheran Theological Seminary cupola. Near the woods to the right is where Maj. Gen. John Reynolds was killed.[3]

In the distance is the railroad cut, appearing like an incision upon the horizon.

11:00 AM

About 500 yards from where Reynolds just fell, several hundred infantrymen from Mississippi and North Carolina believe they have found prime cover—a massive gulley sliced into a hill. Dug months ago in preparation for a rail line, this artificial valley soon proves far too steep and cavernous to be a workable fighting trench. Seeing an opportunity to pin the Southerners in place, New York and Wisconsin regiments promptly rush the position despite fierce volleys spewing from the fold. The Federals have gained positions at the top and east end and are firing into the mass of humanity.

11:15 AM

Just fifteen minutes, and it is all over at the railroad cut. Once the Confederates realized they were trapped, some fought with extreme desperation, others tried to surrender, and still more tried to claw their way up the steep embankments. Losses are extremely heavy on both sides;

Gettysburg, seat of Adams County

nearly a third of the Federals here are killed or wounded, and over half of the Confederates within the trench have been killed, wounded, or captured.[4]

Noon

A lull falls over the field, but not over the horizons. Reinforcements enormous in volume are converging on this place. It appears this poor town is about to become yet another community forcibly hallowed.

12:30 PM

The next mass of Union infantry, the luckless and largely European-born Eleventh Corps, is entering Gettysburg proper from the south. They will have a difficult time navigating the labyrinth of streets, though they have little choice. Descending on them from near Harrisburg is the head of Lee's enormous invasion force, his Second Corps under the capable leadership of Richard Ewell. Old Baldy has some 18,000 men with him, equal in number to the whole

Gettysburg

Seat of Adams County, Pennsylvania

Founded: 1786

Population in 1863: 2,500

Rail Lines: 1 (Gettysburg to Hanover)

Entrance Roads: 10

Buildings: 450

Major Institutions:
Lutheran Theological Seminary (est. 1826)
Gettysburg College (est. 1832)
Gettysburg Female Institute (est. 1856)

Industries and Businesses:
Agriculture, banking, blacksmithing, brick manufacturing, carriage manufacturing, carpentry, education, government, hotels, photography, shoe manufacturing, tanneries, taverns.

Be Advised: Not a "sleepy village." The county seat is essentially a city, with multiple churches, hotels, shops, and warehouses. Tall plank fences, multistory structures, row buildings, plus crisscrossing roads and alleyways are a maze to outsiders. Attempting to maneuver troops through town will be extremely difficult. ■

of the Confederate Army at First Manassas, and the gravity of the situation is pulling them quickly into the fray.

1:30 PM

For the people of Gettysburg, their world seems turned upside down. Not only has the war come to their homes, the South enters from the north, and the North from the south. But there is some good news for the Unionists. The Eleventh Corps has successfully reached the northern edge of town and are spreading out to defend. Unfortunately, the ground is not well suited for such an endeavor, except for a modest knoll about a mile from downtown, and that little bump can hardly hold a half dozen pieces of artillery.

2:00 PM

Robert E. Lee has arrived, and even he feels lost. Of his three gigantic corps, one has been fighting for more than four hours, another is bearing down from the north and about to join the fight, and the third is on the way. Yet Lee's orders are to "avoid a general engagement." Has he lost control? Most vexing

are the unknown whereabouts of Jeb Stuart and his hard-riding cavalry. Without the eyes and ears of these 4,000 horsemen, Lee cannot discern the size and location of the Union's main force.

The news gets worse for the Old Man. As time passes, he hears that Longstreet's First Corps will not reach him for several hours, and some portions are more than a day away. Also, the eager Stuart could be as far as thirty miles distant, possibly conducting one of his famous rides around the opposition. Such antics might play well to the Confederate public, but they could be lethal to the Army of Northern Virginia deep in enemy territory.[5]

3:00 PM

Gettysburg has become a major battle. Confederates are attacking from the west, north, and northeast of town, like a hand clenching down on a skull. The Union First and Eleventh Corps are starting to crack, the former from incessant fighting, the latter from having little suitable high ground from which to defend. Casualties are climbing into the thousands.

The moment necessitates revisiting the term "casualties," because emerging conditions are threatening

Lieutenant General
Richard Stoddard Ewell

Commander, Confederate Second Corps

Age: 46

Nicknames: Old Dick, Baldy, Old Bald Head

Health: Insomnia, migraines, ulcers. Lower right leg amputated after Battle of Second Manassas.

Military Experience: West Point graduate (1840), Mexican War, Native wars, multiple battles in the Eastern Theater.

Strengths: Revered and respected by his officers and men. Intelligent, pragmatic, quick-thinking, listens well to others, understands the strengths and limits of the enlisted.

Weaknesses: At times methodical to a fault. Poor health. Does not care for Lee's vagueness. Lee

wishes Ewell was as aggressive as the man he replaced, the deceased Thomas "Stonewall" Jackson. Susceptible to mood swings.[6] ■

to create a multitude of them. Technically, a casualty is any combatant that has been rendered unable to fight. Most abrupt and complete are those killed in action. Next are the mortally wounded, who reach an aid station before succumbing. Among the living yet compromised are the wounded, sick, or injured.

Then there are the captured or missing, words that are essentially interchangeable because there is no law yet requiring warring parties to report whom they have captured or how many. Nor is there any codification of how POWs are to be treated. Consequently, a soldier taken captive is essentially a disappearance.

4:30 PM

Union corps still on the road cannot reach here in time. Whether Lee wishes to stay is unknown, and at this point his intent hardly matters. His men have pushed the Union First Corps into the shadows of the Seminary buildings and have all but destroyed the Iron Brigade. Ewell and his corps are currently chasing the Federal Eleventh Corps through the streets of town and bagging men by the score. Moreover, the Confederate Army is about to take possession of a northern city.

5:30 PM

The day has become a rout. To bolster Confederate spirits further, Lee's Old War Horse James Longstreet has arrived, and with him stream the first vestiges of the First Corps: Lee's most trusted general leading his largest and strongest fighting arm. The mighty First Corps makes up nearly 40 percent of the Army of Northern Virginia.

Yet it is difficult for anyone to be in a celebratory mood. Across the landscape, medical and burial crews labor in earnest.

7:30 PM

Sunset. Confederate gains are hardly fathomable. Lee appears to have more infantry and artillery present, rare advantages for him. His troops have captured around 3,000 of his enemy, perhaps more, with an equal number killed and wounded. Bluecoats have ceased trying to counterattack. Meade does not appear to be in the area. This is a victory like no other. Tomorrow the grays might very well break the bluecoats altogether, unless there is some unforeseen advantage that the Federals have gained.[7]

Lieutenant General James Longstreet

Commander, Army of Northern Virginia First Corps

Age: 42

Nicknames: Old Pete, Lee's Old War Horse

Health: Excellent, although he (like most of his men) is exhausted from a long and hastened journey to the battle. In the larger context, he is possibly suffering emotional anguish from the brutal, escalating war, as well as from the death of three of his four children the previous year from a scarlet fever epidemic.

Military Experience: West Point graduate (1842), Mexican War, frontier fort service, multiple battles in the Eastern Theater.

Strengths: Intelligent, reliable, even-tempered, aggressive when opportunities emerge. Commands the largest of Lee's three corps, and Lee has almost limitless confidence in his abilities.

Weaknesses: Wisely avoids frontal assaults, but if ordered to do so Longstreet struggles to hide his ambivalence, which may in turn cast doubt in the minds of his subordinates.[8] ■

Night coming on we bivouacked in the streets of the town. . . . The enemy's full force [is] in a commanding position on a high ridge to the southeast of town, strongly entrenched, with artillery in position. The sound of their axes, as they felled abatis, could be heard plainly all night.[9]

> *Confederate soldier in Ramseur's Brigade*

Some of the wounded from the field began to arrive where I was staying. . . . Some limping, some with their heads and arms in bandages, some crawling, others carried on stretchers or brought in ambulances. . . . We were so overcome by the sad and awful spectacle that we hastened back to the house weeping bitterly.[10]

> *Gettysburg resident Tillie Pierce, age 15*

Midnight

The Union's Second, Third, Fifth, and Twelfth Corps start arriving. The Sixth Corps is still a day away. Meade reaches the field and concurs with his subordinates that their current position is good enough. They are going to build up and stay put. Much in line with his character, Meade is avoiding unnecessary risk.

In their favor, Meade and his troops have been forced back onto high ground—mostly hills within close proximity to one another—which should help the Union stabilize their position or at least buy them time.

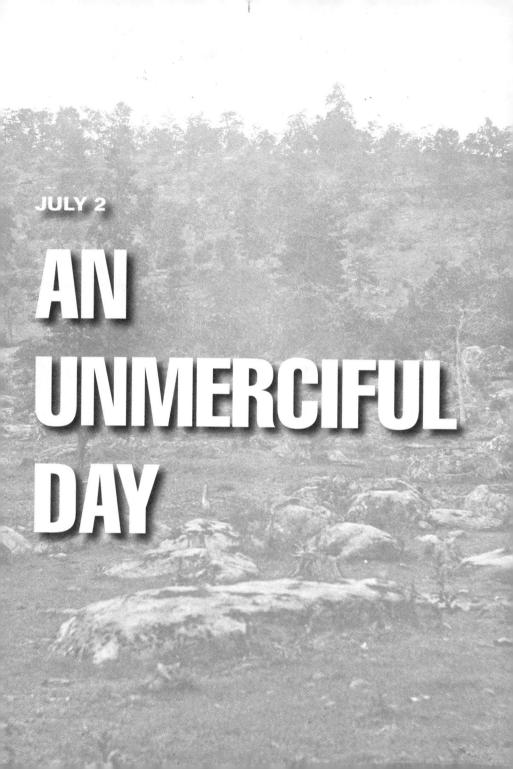

JULY 2

AN UNMERCIFUL DAY

The morning is passing with little more than the sounds of the odd scouting party and the building of hasty breastworks. The Confederates maintain a firm hold on the town and the main tree-lined ridge running south of the Seminary. In contrast, the Federals resemble clumps of driftwood that have been pushed up along the shoreline, as if deposited there by a recent tempest. They lay thick upon a large wooded knoll east of town, with an even heavier concentration on the macabre rise of the town cemetery. Remnants clutter the long crest that stems southward from the graveyard. Two hills anchor the ridge. One is of modest proportions and rocky, while the farther is larger and carpeted with trees. Neither seems particularly usable for military purposes, and as such both hills remain generally unoccupied.

It is probable that the decisive battle is now being fought near Gettysburg.

➤ Evening Courier and Republic,
Buffalo, New York,
July 2, 1863

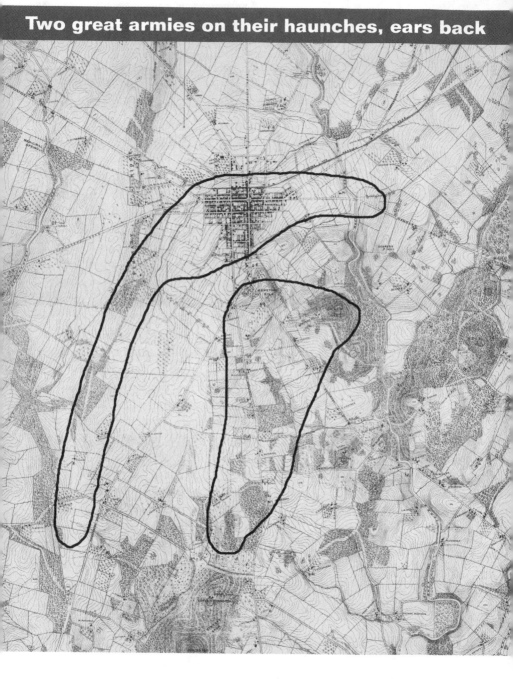

> **There are strong indications tonight that Lee . . . is actually within a short distance of Washington.**
> ➤ Richmond Dispatch,
> *July 2, 1863*

10:00 AM

A very strange absence—there were no journalists here yesterday. A few are starting to make their appearance now, almost exclusively from northern cities.

Common is the dearth of newspapermen at battles west of the Appalachians, where the space between cities is much larger and access to telegraph and rail lines comparatively rare. Here in the urbanizing east, the warring capitals are just one hundred miles apart, and papers far more abundant—Chicago has but four dailies, while New York has eighteen.

Sam Wilkeson of the *New York Times* is on the scene, and for him the battle has become particularly personal. His son Bayard is missing in action and presumed wounded.[1] Tens of thousands of parents are awaiting news of their sons, and theirs will be an equally painful wait. Most reporters are currently in Harrisburg and the surrounding areas, having guessed the main battle would culminate around the state capital, which it may still.

10:30 AM

Even more infantry, cavalry, and artillery arrive, but there is little fighting. It is possible that each side is simply waiting to see what their opponent will do. Federals command the looming hills just south and east of town, plus the long ridge stretching southward from the town cemetery.

Considering Lee's and Meade's mutually impressive defensive positions, this could easily become a standoff. The scenario is likely, considering that Lee must defend his line of retreat to the Shenandoah and Meade is under strict orders to keep himself between the invaders and Washington. Neither army has many options, but who would dare disengage first?

Lee seems to be in the better position overall. He could stay put or pull back into the highly defensible passes of the Shenandoah Mountains and still be in Northern territory. The pressure is on the roughly 90,000 Federals to oust the 70,000 or so Confederates.[2]

Simultaneously, Meade's high ground is impressive if he wishes to use it purely for defensive

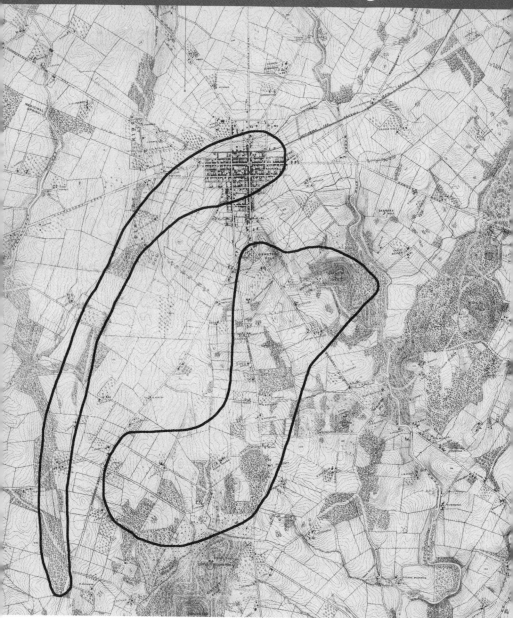

purposes. Some reporters say his army is arranged in the shape of a flattened horseshoe or a long fishhook. A more accurate analogy would be a colossal femur bone. The ball at the hip joint would be the large wooded knob southeast of Gettysburg proper, and the jutting hip would constitute the spanning rise of the town cemetery. Reaching southward from there is the long shank of the bone, low to the ground, until it rises abruptly at the knee joint of two round knolls.

From this vantage, Meade enjoys a much higher position and greater concentration of troops. Lee's line stretches nearly five miles in length to cover this front, while Meade's line is a compact two miles in length.

Noon

Jeb Stuart and his troopers have found their way back to the Army of Northern Virginia, and their comrades cheer upon the reunion. The addition effectively doubles the number of cavalry available to Lee, at a time when he needs reinforcements the most.[3]

1:00 PM

Major components of each army are maneuvering in a most peculiar manner. Longstreet and the Confederate First Corps are filing southward, but at a modest pace, when suddenly they stop and begin to backtrack. Meanwhile the unpredictable Daniel Sickles is ordering his Third Corps forward and away from the relative safety of the Union main line, spreading his troops dangerously thin and protruding them ridiculously westward, as if to invite an attack upon his men. Does either general have the approval of his commander?

I f God gives us Sickles to lead us I shall cry with vexation and sorrow and plead to be delivered.[4]

> *Union Maj. Gen.*
> *Oliver O. Howard*

3:00 PM

The men of Longstreet's First Corps, which is not quite up to full strength, have tired themselves further by resuming their march southward. Apparently, they are accepting Sickles's bizarre invitation to crush his thin and fragmented

Major General Daniel E. Sickles

Commander, Union Third Corps

Age: 43

Nickname: Devil Dan

Health: Contusion from shell fragment at Battle of Chancellorsville.

Military Experience: None.

Strengths: Charismatic, quick study, courageous, devout Unionist.

Weaknesses: Inflated ego, vainglorious. Partial to controversy and prostitutes. No military nor college training. Routinely insubordinate. ■

BRADY-HANDY PHOTOGRAPH COLLECTION, LIBRARY OF CONGRESS

line. But three miles south of Gettysburg seems no place to wage a major contest. The further south one goes, the thicker the woodlands become. Nearer to town is an otherworldly cacophony of enormous boulders, some nearly two stories tall, hardly amenable to orderly lines or artillery caissons. To the east of these behemoths stands a hill too rocky to charge effectively up or down, and a taller sister to its south is too heavily forested to navigate intelligently. As for the fields below, several are merely small pockets cloaked by trees and woven with stone walls and fencerows. It is all a sniper's paradise and a series of traps for larger operations.

4:00 PM

Sunset is less than four hours away, and yet Longstreet's corps has turned eastward. It is going to slam into Sickles's salient. Little good can come of this.

4:15 PM

The Confederates are curling northeast now at the double-quick, as if to deliver a shivering right cross. The first blow is aimed squarely upon a group of Federals wedged between the gigantic boulders and perched atop a hill above.

4:30 PM

Federals on the rocks have managed to deflect much of the first strike, but just to their south a brigade of Alabamians and Texans are marching forward unchecked. If they so choose, these Confederate infantry can make a left turn and get behind the Union holdouts.

Regiments from Michigan, New York, Pennsylvania, and Maine are sprinting to the top of the rocky hill behind this macabre exhibition—perhaps a wise move on their part. The hill could serve as an anchor to their imperiled comrades below. If nothing else, the site is not unlike the weathered remnants of some ancient bastion, virtually worthless as a launching point but sufficient as an ersatz citadel for the moment.

4:45 PM

The Alabama and Texas regiments have made their intentions known. They want the hill and are pressing hard against the lower slopes. They outnumber the Federals two to one and are proceeding with alacrity.

5:30 PM

The fight for the round top begins to resemble a beating heart. Confederate assaults constrict the membrane, and Union counterattacks open its struggling chambers once more. The painful process repeats over and over. Either the heart must rid itself of the blockage or die.

Terrain unsuited for a major engagement, yet both sides are fighting bitterly for this ragged hill south of town that marks the Union left flank. The Union men are holding out, barely, for nearly five hours of intense combat.

Looking northwest toward a peach orchard, with a wheat field 250 yards to the right and out of view.[5]

6:45 PM

A most beautiful peach orchard, perched atop a gentle rise and watching over a handful of idyllic farmsteads in the distance, has become the next of the day's killing fields. This was the most forward position of Sickles's folly, and now it collapses under the weight of superior Confederate numbers.

Arms, heads, legs and parts of dismembered bodies were scattered all about, and sticking among the rocks and against the trunks of trees, hair, brains, entrails and shreds of human flesh.[6]

> ➤ *Union Capt. Robert Carter describing the peach orchard*

One of the worst places to enter in the heat of battle is a wheat field situated in the middle of this ever-growing storm. Tucked into a tree-wrapped valley, it acts like a vortex, pulling regiments into it piecemeal. Few men are making it out alive. It is a place of marginal military importance, but both sides are fighting for it as if the outcome of the war depends upon it. Possession of this acreage is changing hands several times, and the wheat stalks are being cut down to ground level by the thick swarms of bullets flying back and forth. Hardly imaginable, there are already 1,000 casualties, and the number steadily climbs.[7]

Sickles's Corps is collapsing backward to the ridge from whence they came. Reports are that Sickles himself has been severely wounded. The Confederates have broken Sickles's salient, but at horrendous cost. Their casualties exceed 30 percent, and the ground they captured is no more useful to them than it was to their adversaries.

8:15 PM

The news will be hard to bear in and around St. Paul, Minnesota, home of the First Minnesota Regiment. This unit has just lost the majority of its men in less than an hour. They were sent forward from the main Union line to blunt the assault of an entire Confederate brigade (see map on left). Their opponents, almost all of them from Alabama, fared little better. Both came a very long way to be here, and many will never make it back.[8]

8:30 PM

The Confederates are not finished punishing their opponents. Their primary target now is the town cemetery, the most heavily defended Union position on the entire field. Intent on crushing the Federals with envelopment from the west, north, and east are at least eight regiments in gray.

9:00 PM

Cloaked in darkness and rolling smoke, Confederates are pressing ferociously close to the cemetery, and the fighting has turned primal. Unable to reload fast enough, some men are throwing rocks, while others are using the butts of their rifles to club their opponents to death. Yet nothing compares to the damage that the Federal artillery is doing at this point-blank range.

Heads, arms, and legs flying amid the dust and smoke . . . it reminded me much of a wagon load of pumpkins drawn up a hill and the end gate coming out, and the pumpkins rolling and bounding down the hill.[9]

> *Enlisted soldier describing the effects of Union artillery upon Confederate bodies on Cemetery Hill*

10:30 PM

Fighting has slowed, though the countryside is hardly silent; surgical teams continue to work by lamplight. The last of the Confederate First Corps and Union Sixth Corps arrive. Countless wounded cry out from across ten square miles of crags, forests, fields, and ravines, calling for help, water, and home, and not always in that order. The dead number at least 3,000, with the total climbing by the minute as more succumb.

I knelt beside the first man near the door and asked what I could do. "Nothing," he replied, "I am going to die."[10]

> *Gettysburg resident Sallie Myers, tending to the wounded*

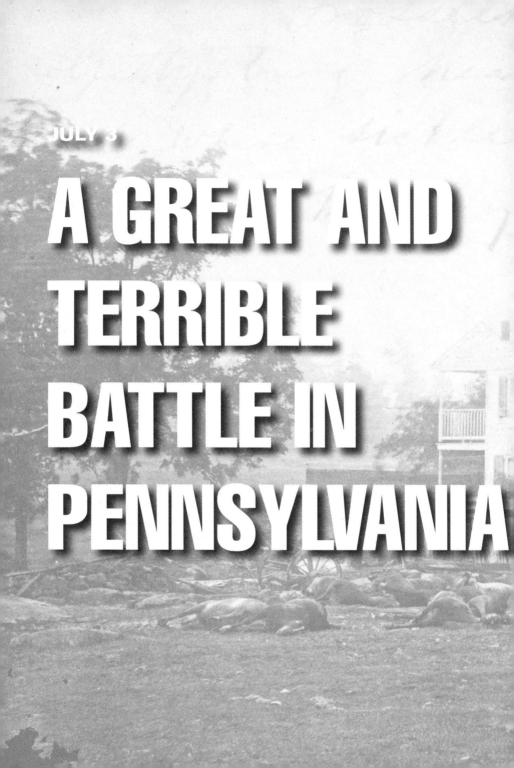

JULY 3

A GREAT AND TERRIBLE BATTLE IN PENNSYLVANIA

4:00 AM

Humid and hazy. Another day of exhausting heat, and the men and horses are already wilting from the long miles covered, brutal fighting endured, and days of sleep lost. If only they could rest.

4:30 AM

Eruption. More than two dozen Federal artillery pieces on and near the wooded hill southeast of town are sending hundreds of shells shrieking into the Confederate left.

5:00 AM

Minutes ago, Confederates charged the wooded hill, presumably to silence the Union guns and seize the high ground. It appears this location might become the epicenter of the day's fight. As it unfolds, the contest resembles the previous day's struggle for the round top south of town: the Union holds the jagged and steep rise, their opponents are sending wave after wave into defended positions, lines are pulsing up and down the hill. The difference now is that somewhere between two and three times as many combatants are involved, and a heavier tree cover intensifies the confusion.

Union dead, and the burial crew waiting to resume their interments.

None but demons can delight in war.[1]

> *Union soldier on Culp's Hill*

9:00 AM

A civilian is dead—a young woman. She was caught in the crossfire between Confederates shooting from homes and alleyways in town and Federal riflemen firing from the cemetery. She may not be the last. Unknown numbers of civilians are still present in the area, having waited too long to evacuate. Pity those just south of town, as their farmsteads are inundated with the dead and dying.

The stench arising from the fields of carnage was most sickening. Dead horses, swollen to almost twice their natural size, lay in all directions, stains of blood frequently met our gaze, and all kinds of army accoutrements covered the ground.[2]

> *Gettysburg resident Tillie Pierce, age 15*

11:00 AM

Fighting around the wooded hill recedes. Only sporadic shots here and there ring out.

Noon

More than 1,000 Confederate horsemen are galloping around Gettysburg's north side. Three thousand more follow in close support. Lee still appears determined to flank the Federals, or at the very least to create an impressive diversion.[3]

Dead horses surround the Trostle family home just north of the wheat field.

1:00 PM

Up to this moment, the battle resembled so many others. Troop movements may appear orderly on field maps or in the imaginations of commanders, but on the ground all fighting becomes personal, broken into fragments, and chaotic.

Yet there is a strangely unified composition developing along the ridge that runs south from the Seminary. A vast host of Confederate batteries are unlimbering in groups of four and six and forming a long, undulating line nearly two miles long. From above, they must look like notes on a long scroll of sheet music. There must be 150 guns in all. The war has not yet seen such an imposing orchestration.

Notably, the instruments are not uniform. Several different types of cannons are visible, indicating a multitude of different calibers. Supplying each with the correct ammunition is going to require a complex arrangement. Whatever ordnance that is available, there cannot be much of it, considering the heated use these barrels experienced in the preceding two days. This all may be for show.[4]

1:10 PM

This is not a show. It is a deafening and deadly unleashing, and the Union crews are responding in kind. The two thundering lines, ranging from a half mile to a mile and a half apart, labor as if they believe they intend to obliterate the other. Each blast feels like a punch to the chest. The air is difficult to breathe, for there is no wind to push away the swirling sulfur. Targets are becoming virtually impossible to see.

The air seemed literally filled with screaming messengers of death.[5]
➤ *Reporter for the* New York Times, *July 4, 1863*

1:20 PM

The Confederate barrage is having marginal effect, partly from low-quality gunpowder, ordnance, and artillery pieces. Cannons are rarely firing the same trajectory twice. Some shots are exploding prematurely, while others aren't detonating at all. Foremost, the majority are overshooting their targets. But all of this may be unknown to the Southern gunners, as powder smoke increasingly envelops each side.[6]

The very earth shook beneath our feet, and the hills and rocks seemed to reel like a drunken man . . . the heavy mutterings from the valley between the opposing armies, the splash of bursting shrapnel, and the fierce neighing of artillery horses, made a picture terribly grand and sublime.[7]

> *Reporter for the* Richmond Enquirer, *July 22, 1863*

1:50 PM

The Confederate bombardment continues, while the Union salvos diminish. The gunners in blue are either running out of ammunition or have decided to be more prudent with their supply.

For God's sake, come quick, or we cannot support you . . . . Ammunition nearly out.[8]

> *Confederate artillery officer E.P. Alexander to Maj. Gen. George Pickett*

2:15 PM

Union artillery has virtually ceased, and Confederate firing rates are slowing. The latter side may be under the false impression that they have successfully destroyed the Union guns, when in fact most are still operable and their crews intact.

2:30 PM

A dogfight has ensued east of town. The 4,000 Confederate cavalry have run headlong into their Union rivals. From a distance, the crack of carbines and swirling sabers make for a frightening scene, but few riders are falling. The terrain prohibits a general engagement. A tight weave of sturdy fencerows frustrates nearly every charge and countercharge. Union batteries and dismounted troops appear to be having the most success, as the fence lines occasionally funnel and clump the Confederates into large and easy targets. One mounted Federal officer appears to be enjoying himself: the youthful, blond Brig. George Armstrong Custer revels in leading his Michigan men in a litany of short, sharp charges.

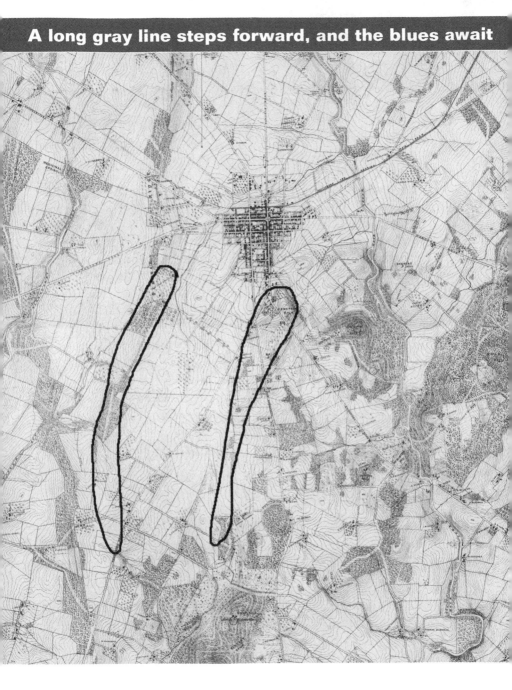

Incomprehensible. Approximately 13,000 Confederate infantry, an army measuring over a mile across, have just stepped from the shadows of their tree line along the Seminary ridge and are heading straight for the Federal defenses. This evokes memories of Longstreet's monstrous assault at Second Manassas. Then again, Old Pete conducted that charge last August with twice as many men, against an exhausted Union flank, with far better artillery support and natural cover. This endeavor will be across nearly a mile of open ground, and evidently only eighteen cannons are rolling forward with him. Two of Longstreet's three divisions consist largely of walking wounded and other survivors of the first two days. Only his recently arrived division under the command of the dapper yet marginally experienced George Pickett is relatively rested and unhurt.[9]

The Army of the Potomac is weary, too, but they hold high ground and wait behind barricades. Perhaps this is just the first wave of a larger Confederate attempt to break through. But do Lee and Longstreet know that the entire Union Sixth Corps has arrived and waits in reserve behind the Union high ground? Should any portion of the attack pierce the Union line, they will be facing a corps nearly as large as this entire Confederate attack.

3:10 PM

Longstreet's assault is nearly halfway across the field, and the Union artillery is upon them. From this distance, batteries on the hills are rendering the worst damage. Fired diagonally across the assault line, Union shells can fall short or long and still hit something. This is lethal crossfire.

Shells amongst us, shells over us and shells around us tore our bleeding ranks with ghastly gaps ... the ground roared and rumbled like a great storm.[10]

> ➤ *Confederate soldier in Pickett's Charge*

3:15 PM

Confederates on the right start to angle inward, overlapping their comrades in the center. The cause is not immediately known, but the effect is terrible confusion. Regiments become enmeshed, making a sluggish and dense target for their adversaries. Chains of command are beginning to stress and break.

3:20 PM

At 200 yards, the Union infantry unleashes a deafening, corrosive volley. Confederates crouch forward, as if walking against a terrible wind. Some of them realize they are under enfilade fire tearing down their length. Union infantry have deployed to their north and south sides and are mowing down each flank. Union artillery has switched from shell to canister—large tin cans filled with boil-sized lead spheres—transforming their tubes into corpulent shotguns. Each successive blast sends limbs and torsos flying.

There was a hissing sound, like the hooded cobra's whisper of death, a deafening explosion . . . and when I got on my feet again there were splinters of bone and lumps of flesh sticking to my clothes.[11]

> ➤ *Col. Joseph Mayo, Army of Northern Virginia*

The next-to-last obstacle: a long rail fence running along the west side of Emmitsburg Road. Individuals position themselves to climb over and push past, exposing the whole of their bodies to incoming fire. For many, the rough-hewn timbers and the Federal line beyond are the last they see of earth.

At 100 yards, those who have made it across start shooting back. Many appear empowered by the effort and they press on. Federal artillerists closest to them fire double canister.

With 50 yards to go, the Confederate assault forms an epicenter, consisting primarily of Virginians to the center right and North Carolinians to the center left. Their final barrier is a long, low stone wall that runs across the Virginians' front, angles 90 degrees back for 100 yards, and then turns 90 degrees again to resume its course.

3:25 PM

The angled wall cleaves the Virginians and Carolinians, with the former slamming against the obstruction and the latter proceeding the 100 yards further. Only a few from Old Dominion make it across, where the fighting turns hand-to-hand. The Tar Heels cannot breech the farther section, gunned down as they are from three directions.[12]

Charlie, the best thing these brave fellows can do is get out of this.[13]

> ➤ *Confederate Maj. Gen. Isaac Trimble to Capt. Charles Grogan*

3:30 PM

Humans cannot long endure this. They fire at each other from point-blank range and club each other with their muskets. A few employ their training and thrust their bayonets deep into abdomens, twisting the blades home.

3:35 PM

In a matter of minutes, every soldier in the immediate area of the wall, North and South, either surrenders, falls wounded, or is killed outright. The Southern tide crashes and ebbs backward, barely half of its original volume. The entire affair creates moer than 6,000 casualties in less than an hour.

4:00 PM

Witnessing the carnage firsthand, and seeing only a few thousand ably return to their line, several of the Confederate officers are visibly distraught. Most try to rally what remains of their units in preparation for a counterattack they assume is coming. From hilltop to hilltop, the Federals shout in triumph, having finally made their rivals fall back in droves.

4:15 PM

The clash of cavalry east of Gettysburg has also burned itself out. Neither side appears successful. More than one hundred dead lie scattered upon the fields. As with all other battles, there will soon come the difficult task of determining who is beyond saving. Humans appraised as doomed will be taken to "dying trees" or some other similarly quiet and shaded area, where they will be kept as comfortable as possible until their time comes.

A most unsettling din emanates from the wounded horses, though their shrill screams wither as their lifeblood flows from bullet holes and severed limbs. Wounded steeds will be placed under the charge of teamsters and horse doctors, where a cursory inspection will decide whether the beast will be spared or shot.[14]

6:00 PM

The Union counterattack is not forthcoming, at least not today, as both sides are physically "fought out." There is much work to do, especially for the surgeons and burial teams.

A survey of the dead between the lines indicates that this battle is like most others in how it kills. Roughly 90 percent of corpses possess bullet wounds; less than 8 percent show signs of artillery impact or mortal concussion from near-hits. Where close-quarter fighting transpired, fractured skulls and powder burns are somewhat common. Very few seem to have been killed by an edged weapon.

Regardless of the device, the site of entry clearly played a primary role in deciding the fate of the recipient. Eighty percent of the dead have holes and lacerations to the neck and head. About 15 percent have been struck in the chest or stomach. Only about 5 percent of the deceased were hit exclusively in a limb, where presumably the bullet or shell fragment severed an artery.

At the field hospitals, of which there are many, the numbers are largely inversed. Most of the wounded are hit in a limb and are still alive at the moment, whereas very few survivors have head and neck wounds.[15]

The burden now falls upon comrades, officers, nurses, and journalists to gather what information is known and report accordingly to families back home, although the anxious and chaotic atmosphere hardly fosters accurate accounts as to who has been lost and who is still among the living.

Longstreet was mortally wounded and captured. He is reported to have died an hour afterward. Also, some twenty thousand Confederates were believed captured, with the Union cavalry encircling the rest.[16]

➣ New York Times, *July 6, 1863*

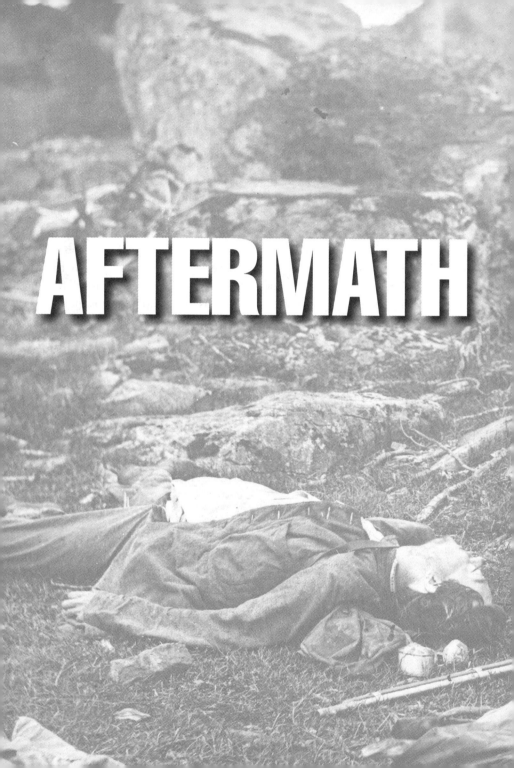

AFTERMATH

July 4

There are no fireworks today, celebratory or otherwise. Rain falls in torrents from a gloomy sky. Confederates are pulling back, and the Federals are making few attempts to follow, largely because they don't want to duplicate Lee's mistake of yesterday—making a frontal assault over open ground.

July 5

Both sides are pulling away, and they are leaving behind a haunting dystopia.

Astride a tree sat a **bloody horror, with head and limbs severed by shells, the birds having banqueted on it, while the tattered uniform, stained with gore, fluttered dismally in the summer air. Whole bodies were flattened against the rocks, smashed into a shapeless mass, as though thrown there by a giant hand.**[1]
➤ *Volunteer nurse Sophronia Bucklin*

A group of three photographers are here. They are working primarily around the farmsteads and the strange assemblage of massive boulders south of town, capturing images of the mangled men and animals. Lately they seem to be getting creative with their subjects, laying a rifle upon a corpse or arranging a few accoutrements and tree limbs around the bodies to ornament the scene. On occasion, they drag the deceased for a few yards in search of a more compelling backdrop. These artists have many portraits from which to choose. The dead alone outnumber residents three to one. A resident of the Evergreen Cemetery's arched gatehouse is helping to bury the scattered dead around her home, and she is six months pregnant.[2]

Of far greater concern to the citizens are the wounded: the ratio to the local population is almost ten to one, and pitifully few military doctors are present to treat them. Evidently, both Lee and Meade anticipate a much larger fight to come, so both are departing with approximately 80 percent of their medical teams, ambulances, operating equipment, hospital tents, and supplies, leaving just 160 Confederate and Union surgeons to care for 24,000 bleeding bodies.[3]

By necessity and often through their own volition, citizens are taking the wounded into their homes and providing for them as best as possible. Other civilians are being commandeered. During one amputation in a private home, a doctor solicits the help of one of the occupants, a common occurrence now, although in this case the person deputized is a ten-year-old girl.[4]

Without question, time is a factor. Surgeries conducted within the first twenty-four hours tend to save the patient, while those performed seventy-two hours after injury are rarely successful.

July 8

News comes that the Union has taken Vicksburg. If the war is to have a turning point, this may very well be it. The Mississippi belongs to the Federals, as do most of the major rivers, roads, and railways now. Whether events in this southern Pennsylvania town will have any lasting effect seems unlikely, although both sides are claiming a great victory.

Four federal generals were killed, and General G. Meade, the new commander in place of Hooker, is said to have been severely wounded . . . the Confederates achieved a victory at Gettysburg.[5]
➤ North Carolina Standard, *Raleigh, North Carolina, July 8, 1863*

Photo taken July 6 by Lawrence Gardner and Timothy O'Sullivan after they arranged military equipment around a body for dramatic effect.[6]

All the news from the vicinity of Gettysburg . . . confirms the fact that the defeat of General Lee's army on Friday was a total rout.

➤ Reading Times, *Reading, Pennsylvania, July 8, 1863*

In Gettysburg, philanthropic organizations and citizens alike are working to repair the harm wrought by warring governments. Hundreds of workers from the United States Christian Commission are here, as are the Ladies Aid Society of Philadelphia, the Catholic Sisters of Mercy, the New York Soldiers' Relief Agency, and many

AFTERMATH

others. They bring several tons of fresh vegetables, butter, eggs, milk, flour, and poultry, plus mountains of blankets, a forest of crutches, and imperial tons of clean clothes—all private donations. Volunteer nurses and doctors tend to the sick and injured. Cooks and bakers concoct thousands of hot meals and fresh loaves of bread. For all the carnage that the battle wrought, the warring parties came and left with relative haste, leaving much of the region's infrastructure in place and able to service the people in need.[7]

With the assistance of others in the area, Sam Wilkeson of the *New York Times* has found his son Bayard. The young lieutenant lies dead in a shallow grave, having succumbed to arterial wounds he received while trying to defend Gettysburg on July 1. His mourning father reflects upon what has happened and tells his readers that he hopes the loss of so many sons will somehow grant the nation "a second birth of freedom."[8]

August 20

After mutual declarations of victory, Unionists and Confederates alike are starting to wonder if the contest here was at best a draw. Reportedly, both Meade and Lee have offered their resignations. Their respective commanders-in-chief publicly offer praise but are privately shocked by the enormous losses.

I do not believe you appreciate the magnitude of the misfortune involved in Lee's escape. He was within your easy grasp, and to have closed upon him would, in connection with our other late successes, have ended the war. As it is, the war will be prolonged indefinitely. . . . Your golden opportunity is gone, and I am distressed immeasurably because of it.[9]

➢ *Letter from Lincoln to Meade, never signed, never sent*

We have suffered a check.[10]

➢ *Jefferson Davis*

It is going to take many months to calculate how many soldiers have been lost, and the precise totals may never be known. However, indications are that this battle is not only the largest and deadliest of the war so far, it has also been the largest and costliest ever to transpire in the history of North America.

U.S. Sanitary Commission, Gettysburg, August 1863. The civilian commission and other philanthropies arrived hours after the battle when the warring parties could not or would not fully care for the dead and injured left behind.

Altogether, three days of fighting have reduced the Army of Northern Virginia's ranks by more than 30 percent. No other engagement has scythed their numbers so severely. The Army of the Potomac has lost nearly 25 percent of its men, making this battle among its most lethal undertakings.[11]

The casualties at Gettysburg were doubtless the heaviest on both sides that have yet been sustained. The most intense anxiety is manifested throughout all portions of the country to know the particulars, extent of our loss, etc., and it is strange that but little or indefinite accounts have yet been received.[12]

> ➤ Western Sentinel, *Winston, North Carolina, July 17, 1863*

Spare a thought for the families awaiting word of their loved ones in uniform. For some, news will never arrive, denying them a sense of closure. Others will hear that their son or brother has died. Even then, nearly a third of Federal deceased and more than half of Confederate dead are interred in unmarked graves, denying this form of closure as well. Many a family will see their soldier boy again, only to find that he has lost something of himself: physically, mentally, or both.

For all its cost, has this fight brought an end to the war? For now, the most likely outcome of the Battle of Gettysburg and for its residents is the establishment of yet another "national cemetery" in the near future. As for the rest of the country, they may struggle to comprehend just what happened here for generations to come.

Notes

Spring 1863: An Intensifying Nightmare

1. For issues of the blockade, see Mark E. Neely, Jr., "The Perils of Running the Blockade: The Influence of International Law in an Era of Total War," *Civil War History* 32 (1986).

2. Lincoln quoted in Michael Burlingame, *Abraham Lincoln: A Life* (Baltimore: Johns Hopkins University Press, 2012), 498.

3. For details on Southern food shortages and their causes, see James M. McPherson, *Battle Cry of Freedom* (New York: Oxford University Press, 1988), 384, 440; Dorothy and James Volo, *Daily Life in the Civil War* (Westport, CT: Greenwood, 1998), 230–34.

4. *The War of the Rebellion: A Compilation of the Official Records of the Union and Confederate Armies* (Washington, DC: Government Printing Office, 1899), Ser. 1, Vol. 27, pt. 3, p. 27 (hereafter referred to as *O.R.*). Lincoln quoted in Brooks D. Simpson, *The Civil War in the East: Struggle, Stalemate, and Victory* (Santa Barbara: Praeger, 2011), 77.

5. *New York Herald*, May 30, 1863, p. 6.

6. *Memphis Appeal* (Atlanta, GA), July 6, 1863, p. 2.

7. *Alexandria Gazette* (Alexandria, VA), May 29, 1863, p. 4.

8. *Richmond Enquirer*, July 3, 1863, p. 1.

9. *Mobile Daily Advertiser and Register* (Mobile, AL), June 20, 1863, quoted in J. Cutler Andrews, *The South Reports the Civil War* (Princeton: Princeton University Press, 1970), 307.

10. Allan Nevins, *The War for the Union: The Organized War, 1863–1864* (New York: Charles Scribner's Sons, 1971), 80.

11. *O.R.*, Ser. 1, Vol. 27, pt. 1, p. 50.

12. *Caledonian Mercury* (Edinburgh, Scotland), July 1, 1863, p. 2.

13. McPherson, 649.

14. Confederate soldier quoted in William Hassler, *A.P. Hill: Lee's Forgotten General* (Richmond: Garrett and Massie, 1957), 150.

15. Bureau of the Census, *Manufactures of the United States in 1860; Compiled from the Returns of the Eighth Census* (Washington, DC: Government Printing Office, 1865), 538–44; Joseph T. Glatthaar, "The Common Soldier's Gettysburg Campaign," in *The Gettysburg Nobody Knows*, ed. Gabor Boritt (New York: Oxford University Press, 1997), 9; Bureau of the Census, *Agriculture of the United States in 1860; Compiled from the Returns of the Eighth Census* (Washington, DC: Government Printing Office, 1864), 121–25.
16. O.R., Ser. 1, Vol. 27, pt. 3, p. 369.
17. O.R., Ser. 1, Vol. 27, pt. 3, p. 426.
18. Edwin B. Coddington, *The Gettysburg Campaign: A Study in Command* (New York: Charles Scribner's Sons, 1984), 173–75.
19. Glatthaar, 9.

July 1: Contact and Escalation

1. Sadie Bushman quoted in Jim Slade and John Alexander, *Firestorm at Gettysburg* (Atglen, PA: Schiffer, 1998), 53.
2. Reynolds quoted in Edwin B. Coddington, *The Gettysburg Campaign: A Study in Command* (New York: Charles Scribner's Sons, 1984), 269.
3. William Frassanito, *Gettysburg: A Journey in Time* (New York: Charles Scribner's Sons, 1975), 60–69.
4. Lance R. Herdegen and William K. Beaudot, *In the Bloody Railroad Cut at Gettysburg* (Dayton, OH: Morningside House, 1990), 211.
5. Noah Trudeau, *Gettysburg: A Testing of Courage* (New York: Harper Collins, 2002), 212–18.
6. O.R., Ser. I, Vol. 27, pt. 2, p. 317; Donald C. Pfanz, *Richard S. Ewell: A Soldier's Life* (Chapel Hill: University of North Carolina Press, 1998), 303.
7. Coddington, 309–11.
8. Jeffry D. Wert, *General James Longstreet* (New York: Simon and Schuster, 1993), 256–60.
9. Letter from soldier in Ramseur's Brigade written to his own mother and wife, July 8, 1863, quoted in *Daily Progress* (Raleigh, NC), July 22, 1863, p. 2.
10. E.F. Conklin, *The Women at Gettysburg, 1863* (Gettysburg, PA: Thomas Publications, 1993), 88.

July 2: An Unmerciful Day

1. News of Lt. Bayard Wilkeson's wounding and capture reported in "The Battle of Wednesday," *New York Times*, July 4, 1863, p. 1.

2. Alan T. Nolan makes the valid observation that Lee had the option to pull back to Cashtown, which would have provided the Army of Northern Virginia with better supply lines, an impressively strong defensive position, and a quick escape option, all while keeping the pressure upon Meade to oust his army from Pennsylvania. See Nolan, *Lee Considered: General Robert E. Lee and Civil War History* (Chapel Hill: University of North Carolina Press, 1991), 96–99. Harry W. Pfanz notes that the option to stay in place at Gettysburg was also a viable and sustainable choice for Lee, as it gave his army access to the town and its supplies, a defensive ridge, command of several roads, and an enemy countryside from which he could continue foraging. See Pfanz, *Gettysburg: The Second Day* (Chapel Hill: University of North Carolina Press, 1987), 164–67.

3. Allen C. Guelzo makes the compelling point that evidence is sparse regarding Lee's demeanor toward Stuart upon the latter's arrival at Gettysburg. Whether Lee was upset or not, the commander still had several thousand troopers with him before Stuart rejoined him. See, Guelzo, *Gettysburg: The Last Invasion* (New York: A.A. Knopf, 2013), 362–63.

4. Howard quoted in Edwin B. Coddington, *The Gettysburg Campaign: A Study in Command* (New York: Charles Scribner's Sons, 1984), 37.

5. William Frassanito, *Gettysburg: A Journey in Time* (New York: Charles Scribner's Sons, 1975), 196–207.

6. Capt. Robert G. Carter quoted in *War Papers Read before the Commandery of the State of Maine, Vol. 2* (Portland, ME: Lefavor-Tower, 1902), 181.

7. Calculations of the Wheatfield killed and wounded include the immediately adjacent areas of the Peach Orchard and part of Plum Run Valley that lies just south of the Wheatfield road. Total losses in this sector are estimated to be 1,754 over 80 acres. See John Busey and David Martin, *Regimental Strengths and Losses at Gettysburg* (Highstown, NJ: Longstreet House, 1986), 245, 247, 282; Pfanz, 370.

8. Richard Moe, *The Last Full Measure: The Life and Death of the First Minnesota Volunteers* (New York: Henry Holt, 1993), 8. In total regimental losses at Gettysburg, the 1st Minnesota only ranks sixteenth, yet

this is due in large part to the regiment's small number at the start of the battle.

9. Private witnessing the effect of Cemetery Hill Union artillery fire on the night of July 2 quoted in Bradley M. Gottfried, *The Maps of Gettysburg* (New York: Savas Beatie, 2007), 218.

10. Sallie Myers quoted in Jim Slade and John Alexander, *Firestorm at Gettysburg* (Atglen, PA: Schiffer, 1998), 76.

July 3: A Great and Terrible Battle in Pennsylvania

1. L.R. Coy of the 123rd New York and S.R. Norris of the 7th Ohio quoted in John M. Archer, *Culp's Hill at Gettysburg* (Gettysburg, PA: Thomas Publications, 2002), 121.

2. E.F. Conklin, *The Women at Gettysburg, 1863* (Gettysburg, PA: Thomas Publications, 1993), 92.

3. Gary Kross, "True Cavalry: Jeb Stuart and George Custer at Gettysburg," *Blue and Gray Magazine* (July 1997), 50.

4. Gregory Coco, *A Concise Guide to the Artillery at Gettysburg* (Gettysburg, PA: Thomas Publications, 1998), 84–85; Earl Hess, *Pickett's Charge: The Last Attack at Gettysburg* (Chapel Hill: University of North Carolina Press, 2001), 25, 117.

5. *New York Times*, July 4, 1863.

6. Fairfax Downey, *The Guns of Gettysburg* (New York: David McKay Company, 1958), 133; Jeffrey C. Hall, *The Stand of the U.S. Army at Gettysburg* (Bloomington: Indiana University Press, 2003), 190.

7. *Daily Richmond Enquirer*, July 22, 1863.

8. Alexander quoted in Lesley J. Gordon, *General George E. Pickett in Life and Legend* (Chapel Hill: University of North Carolina Press, 1998), 111.

9. Edwin B. Coddington, *The Gettysburg Campaign: A Study in Command* (New York: Charles Scribner's Sons, 1984), 68; Jeffrey D. Wert, *Gettysburg: Day Three* (New York: Simon and Schuster, 2001), 128.

10. Confederate soldier's account of artillery barrage during Pickett's Charge from Bradley M. Gottfried, *The Maps of Gettysburg* (New York: Savas Beatie, 2007), 208.

11. Col. Joseph Mayo quoted in Richard Rollins, ed., *Pickett's Charge: Eyewitness Accounts* (Redondo Beach, CA: Rank & File Publ., 994), 147.

12. Carol Reardon, *Pickett's Charge in History and Memory* (Chapel Hill: University of North Carolina Press, 2001), 32.
13. Trimble quoted in Kent Masterson Brown, *Retreat from Gettysburg: Lee, Logistics, and the Pennsylvania Campaign* (Chapel Hill: University of North Carolina Press, 2005), 2.
14. Kross, 50.
15. George W. Adams, *Doctors in Blue: The Medical History of the Union Army in the Civil War* (Baton Rouge: Louisiana State University, 1952), 115.
16. *New York Times*, July 6, 1863.

Aftermath

1. Bucklin quoted in Gregory A. Coco, *A Strange and Blighted Land* (Gettysburg, PA: Thomas Publications, 1995), 20.
2. Margaret S. Creighton, *The Colors of Courage: Immigrants, Women, and African Americans in the Civil War's Defining Battle* (Cambridge, MA: Basic Books, 2005), 96, 120.
3. Gregory Coco estimates around a hundred U.S. ambulances (about 10 percent) remained behind at Gettysburg, while Gerard Patterson suggests perhaps thirty remained. Coco, 54, 158; Gerald Patterson, *Debris of Battle: The Wounded of Gettysburg* (Mechanicsburg, PA: Stackpole Books, 1997), 110.
4. Creighton, 118–19.
5. "Latest News—Battle of Gettysburg," *North Carolina Standard* (Raleigh, NC), July 8, 1863.
6. William Frassanito, *Gettysburg: A Journey in Time* (New York: Charles Scribner's Sons, 1975), 186–191.
7. Coco, 240–46; Jim Slade and John Alexander, *Firestorm at Gettysburg* (Atglen, PA: Schiffer, 1998), 161.
8. Account of Lieutenant Wilkeson's death from Harold Holzer, *Lincoln and the Power of the Press: The War for Public Opinion* (New York: Simon and Schuster, 2015), 433–34; and Michael A. Dreese, *Torn Families: Death and Kinship at the Battle of Gettysburg* (Jefferson, NC: McFarland, 2007), 11–12.
9. Lincoln quoted in Benjamin P. Thomas, *Lincoln: A Biography* (New York: The Modern Library, 1968), 389.

10. Davis quoted in Herman Hattaway and Richard E. Beringer, *Jefferson Davis, Confederate President* (Lawrence: University of Kansas Press, 2002), 232.

11. Lee's offer of resignation in Michael Fellman, *The Making of Robert E. Lee* (New York: Random House, 2000), 147–149, 151. Meade's offer of resignation in *O.R.*, Ser. I, Vol. 27, pt. 1, pp. 92–94.

12. "The News," *Western Sentinel* (Winston, NC), July 17, 1863, p. 2.

Suggested Reading

The Colors of Courage: Immigrants, Women, and African Americans in the Civil War's Defining Battle by Margaret S. Creighton. Creighton's monograph is one of the first to recognize how the engagement encompassed the whole of the region's population, and how the war itself was part of an international phenomenon.

Gettysburg by Stephen W. Sears. A highly approachable narrative overview.

Gettysburg: A Journey in Time by William A. Frassanito. A breakthrough study of early photojournalism and how individual images can shape collective memory. Frassanito's "then-and-now" images have become even more compelling over time, as his mid-1970s photos show how the battlefield has changed in the last fifty years as well.

The Gettysburg Campaign: A Study in Command by Edwin B. Coddington. The gold standard overview, highly detailed, with emphases on troop movements and command decisions.

Gettysburg: Memory, Market, and an American Shrine by Jim Weeks. An engaging and scholarly explanation of how a site of horror became a national treasure, then a family vacation destination, and eventually a haven for reflection and dialogue.

The Gettysburg Nobody Knows, edited by Gabor Boritt. Several of the most noted scholars of the battle offer insight on a rich variety of illuminating topics, from the experience of the average soldier, to reasons why Pickett's Charge failed, to legacy and memorials.

Gettysburg: The Second Day by Harry W. Pfanz. Most historians agree the second day was militarily the most significant, and this volume brings detail and clarity to those impactful twenty-four hours like no other examination.

Gettysburg: The Story of the Battle with Maps by David Reisch and David M. Detweiler. A vivid journey for the visual learner, this atlas shows how the fight unfolded and the fundamental role of landscapes in the battle's devolution.

Guide to Gettysburg Battlefield Monuments by Tom Huntington. Locations and descriptions of every monument and tablet located in the Battlefield Park, conveniently organized by state.

The History Buff's Guide to Gettysburg by Thomas R. Flagel and Ken Allers, Jr. A collection of annotated, detailed top-ten lists, including Lee's motives for invasion, the best and worst performing commanders, local heroines, and the deadliest sections of the battlefield.

Retreat from Gettysburg: Lee, Logistics, and the Pennsylvania Campaign by Kent Masterson Brown. An engineering perspective on combat operations, Brown's study profoundly demonstrates how complex and chaotic Civil War campaigns could be.

A Strange and Blighted Land by Gregory A. Coco. The leading researcher on the conflict's pathos, Coco does his best work on this assessment of the engagement's lasting damage.

War, Memory, and the 1913 Gettysburg Reunion by Thomas R. Flagel. An examination of the largest Blue and Gray reunion ever, revealing that while politicians gave speeches praising nationalism, martyrdom, and death, veterans sought personal connections and confirmation of life.